I Hate School

Claudine G. Wirths & Mary Bowman-Kruhm

HOW TO HANG IN
& WHEN TO DROP OUT

illustrations by Patti Stren

A Harper Trophy Book

Harper & Row, Publishers

Library of Congress Cataloging-in-Publication Data
Wirths, Claudine G.
   I hate school

   Summary: A self-help manual for the potential high
school dropout, discussing how to improve study skills,
handle various school-related problems, and decide
whether dropping out is the best solution.
   1. School attendance—High school—Juvenile
literature.   2. High school dropouts—Juvenile
literature.   3. Study, Method of—Juvenile literature.
4. Reading comprehension—Juvenile literature.
[1. Study, Method of.   2. Dropouts.   3. High schools]
I. Bowman-Kruhm, Mary.   II. Stren, Patti, ill.
III. Title.
LC142.W57   1986   373.12′913   85-48248
ISBN 0-690-04556-5
ISBN 0-690-04558-1 (lib. bdg.)

   (A Harper Trophy book)
ISBN 0-06-446054-1 (pbk.)

This book is dedicated to our husbands, Theodore and Carl,
and to our children: William Wirths, David Wirths,
Hope McGonigle, Bonnie Redmond and Jean Theofield.

C.G.W.

M.B.-K.

To the one person who always hung in there
with me—my brother David.
And to everyone who rejected my drawings
and told me I'd never get published,
making me so angry that I sat in my room
and I drew and I drew and I drew
and I didn't drop out and I didn't give up!!

P.S.

CONTENTS

I Hate School

INTRODUCTION
WHO
ARE
YOU?

Who are you?

We wish we could ask you this question face to face, because we'd like to know you better.

We are a couple of teachers who understand that not everybody likes school. We wrote this book for all of you who are just barely passing because you don't particularly want to study or because you don't find that the studying you do seems to pay off. We have known a good many people like you and here's what we have found.

You aren't dumb. You are often a lot of fun and very creative. Some of you could do really well in school if you wanted to—but right now you don't want to. Some of you have a hard time doing well in school because you have problems with

things like reading, writing reports, and taking tests. All of you have hassles over homework. Every one of you would like to have a diploma, but not all of you are sure you want to do what is necessary to get one.

There are lots of reasons why you could be turned off to school, and we don't think this book is going to make you love school and get on the honor roll. But we can show you some tricks to get better grades. We can show you how to learn more in the time you do study. We can help you decide what homework you have to do and what you can let slide. We can help you read better and faster. We can help you write good reports in the shortest possible time, and we can help you remember things more easily.

Most important of all, we can help you take control of your school life and help you be in charge of what happens to you from now on.

Give us a try. What have you got to lose? You can always go back to failing or dropping out. In fact, in this book we will talk about when it might be smart for you to drop out and get on with a job.

Sound interesting? Read on—we'd like to think you'll feel pretty good about yourself when you finish reading this book.

1
WHAT TO DO
IF YOU HATE SCHOOL

So you hate school? Well, maybe you don't *hate* it, but you sure don't look forward to getting up in the morning and spending the day in school.

How can I keep my mind on school when I can't stop worrying?

Don't even try. Go right to the last chapter of this book. Look for some places to go for help and get started working on what's worrying you.

As soon as you start getting some help, turn back to the chapters in this book on homework and test taking. They will help you keep up with your schoolwork even when you aren't giving it your best. The important thing is, *go get help now!*

That's not my problem. I hate school because I never seem to get the hang of it. What do teachers want, anyway?

Sounds like you really try, but that you need to know how to study better and faster. Skip the rest of this chapter for now and start looking at the chapters on reading, writing, and test taking. You will be amazed at how much easier some of your schoolwork will become when you learn to study smarter—not longer.

Then read this chapter to help you understand more about why school is a problem for you. It will help you know more about what teachers want, too.

Well, I hate school. It is boring and dumb. I don't see why I have to go. I figure this book is just one more way of trying to *make* me go.

Why do you let other people run your life? Nobody can *make* you do anything. You do have choices, you know. If you are old enough to drop out (age sixteen in most states), you can choose to stay in school, or you can choose to drop out and get a job or try living off your folks. If you are still underage, you have another choice: You can do absolutely nothing with the time you have left in school, or you can try and make the most of it. The point is, *you are the one who decides to go to school or to make school worth your while.*

But people are always on my back about staying in school and getting good grades. So what difference do those choices make to me?

They make a big difference. Once you realize you aren't a little kid anymore and that you have control of your life, you can stop feeling pushed and pulled around. You can know why you do what you do.

We guess that right now sometimes you do homework and sometimes you don't, but you don't know why. You tend to blame the teacher for giving you too much, or your friends for asking you out, or your folks for bugging you when you don't do it. The truth is, *you* are the one who decides whether you will do the homework or whether you won't—no matter how much there is or what your folks or friends do or say.

The bad thing about not realizing that you are in charge is that you are always under attack from somebody—your family, your friends, your teachers—all saying what you should do. If you just drift, letting first one person and then another push you or pull you, you could go along for years and not get anywhere. Do you know that you could keep on "sort of" going to school for years, waste all that time you have already put in and still end up with no diploma, no knowledge, and nothing to show for it but a lot of memories of bad times?

I think you're still giving me the same old line. Are you saying that I should just go on to school, spend hours studying, and make the honor roll? No way!

You *might* choose to do that. We don't really know. We can't tell you just what is best for you. What might be best for you is to drop out—honestly. We can talk about that next. The important thing for you to do right now is to make up your mind to take your schoolwork and your education into your own hands and decide what they mean in your life now and what they will mean later. You need to know what your choices are and what is likely to happen to you once you do make a choice.

I've made my choice. I'm planning to drop out at the end of this year. What do you think of that?

School isn't for everybody, but if you aren't going to school, you need a plan. Instead of "dropping out," you need to "step out." You need to step out of school and into a job or some training that will give you a job you want someday.

Here are some things to think about when you consider dropping out. See if these are things you can agree are important.

- *If you are over sixteen, more than two years older than most of the other students in your grade, and failing in*

most of your classes even though you put in a good bit of time on homework and don't skip many classes, you may be better off planning a career for yourself. Don't drop out until you find a place that will hire and train you, and has room for you to move up. Remember, you are looking for a lifetime skill that will bring you enough money to live on comfortably.

- If you need to work full time to help your folks make enough to live on—not just to buy snacks and extras— don't drop out until you find a good job and have talked to your counselor about going to night school. It is hard to push yourself to go to school and study nights and weekends, but you can do it if you want to get a diploma. If night school won't work, ask your school counselor about Saturday school or about taking the G.E.D. (General Educational Development) exam.

What's the G.E.D.?

The G.E.D. is a state exam. If you pass it, you get a certificate saying you passed an exam equal to the requirements for a high school diploma. Your school counselor can tell you all about it. Make no mistake, though—this is a very hard exam. You will have to study for it. Some communities offer night classes to help you study. But think about this: If you can't push yourself to do your homework now, what makes you think you could push yourself to study for the G.E.D.?

Some colleges and most employers will accept a G.E.D. certificate in place of a diploma, so if you do decide to drop out, at least give the G.E.D. a try.

I may drop out because I may flunk out.

Why are you flunking out? Have you quit trying to study because you think working would be easier and more fun than going to school? If so, you need to talk to some young people four or five years older than you who dropped out before they finished high school. Find out how they're doing, what kind of money they make, and who their friends are. Ask them if they wish they had stayed in school. Give yourself at least one grading period of time for talking to people and checking out the idea before you drop out. During that time use some of the ideas in this book to help you keep your grades up in case you decide to stay in.

Are your grades falling because you're always breaking school rules? Most young people find that school, even with all its rules, is a better place to be than just on the street with no good job and no education. If you decide to drop out for a while to get away from rules, talk with your school principal and be sure you can get back in if you change your mind.

Are your grades falling because you're on drugs? Be honest with yourself. Have you recently begun taking drugs or

has your use of drugs, including alcohol, increased over the last year? If your answer is yes to either question, your real problem may be your need for drugs, not your schoolwork. Try going absolutely clean of all drugs for thirty days. If you find that you cannot, you have a problem. It is as simple as that and you need help right away, even if you don't think you do. When your grades fall off after you start taking drugs, you aren't taking drugs, they are taking you. Go to your school counselor today or get in touch with one of the groups listed in the last chapter of this book. What have you got to lose?

I guess I'm just tired of school.

If you are tired of school and want a break from doing the same old thing day after day, why not get a part-time job?

It may take you longer to graduate, but it could change your feelings about going to school. Don't forget, though, a part-time job may mean you have to forget afterschool activities.

You say you don't take part in any afterschool activities? That could be part of your problem. When you join a club or a team, it wakes up your interest in school. If your school says you have to keep up a C average to be in a club, it helps give you the push to do better work to stay in the club.

If you have never joined any school club, try the group that puts on plays. There is a need there for whatever you do best, from being on stage to painting scenery to running the lights or just cleaning up. They need people who can do carpentry and people who like makeup or who can sew costumes.

Ask some other students; they'll tell you school isn't so bad when you have something or someone to look forward to at school every day. You might even find a teacher who likes the same kind of music you do and will help you start a music club. You would be surprised at the different interests teachers have. In almost any junior or senior high there are teachers who like cars, motorcycles, all kinds of music, cooking, computers, camping, hunting, dancing, or reading. Ask around and you may be surprised.

Don't just drop out and go to work to keep from being bored—don't forget, you will probably work nine to five until you are sixty-five. That can get boring. And the way to keep that from getting boring is to get enough education to learn a career skill that is just right for you!

My dad dropped out of school and he has done okay. Why won't he let me?

Twenty years ago it was quite possible to begin a job with a great future without a high school degree. Today there are very few jobs like that. Jobs that don't require any education today are usually dead-end jobs. After twenty years you would probably be making very little more money than you did at the start.

To drop out successfully, you have to plan very carefully and be able to go into a trade or craft that trains you on the job. It's hard work and there aren't many openings in today's job market. Your dad is just being realistic.

Aw, I'm just too dumb to graduate. I'll never make it anyway. Why should I keep on trying?

In the first place, we have known some students who were truly very limited in their ability to think and study, but they worked hard, kept at it, and graduated just fine. Anyone who works hard, does homework every night, and doesn't cut classes has a good chance of making it.

If you have a very hard time reading and writing, you may have a learning disability. If you have spent your whole life feeling like you should be able to do better, but no matter how hard you try you still can't seem to learn the same way other people do, you might need some very special help. Talk to your school counselor, your school's reading teacher, or the school psychologist if you have one. Tell them how the problem looks to you and ask for some help. You can find some other places to get help in the last chapter of this book. Good luck! We believe you are smart, even though it is hard to prove it to other people. Some very famous people have had the same problem, so you are not alone. Keep trying until you get some help.

I don't want to be in some special ed class. The other kids call you "retard" and "dummy" and other stuff. I'd rather flunk out than be in special ed.

You bring up a good point. We know some students who have been in special ed classes and have been popular at school and done just fine. We asked them what they would say to you. Here's what they said:

"Don't let other people know it bothers you. Just ignore most of the cracks. Don't fight unless you absolutely have to. If you need the help, just be glad there is someone who will help you. The kids who are afraid to get help won't laugh when they flunk out and you graduate. Try to get your coun-

selor to put you in some regular classes. You may have to work extra hard, but it's worth it."

I don't know what's the matter with me. My folks say I'm smart, but I don't think I'm all that smart. In a way I'm scared to try to make good grades.

This happens. There are all kinds of personal reasons for being afraid to make good in school or for wanting to fail. Some people are afraid that if they do well people will expect too much of them. Other people want to fail in order to hurt somebody who cares about whether or not they fail. Sometimes students fail just to get some attention. If any of these problems sound familiar to you, go talk to your counselor or to a psychologist or social worker. You shouldn't feel like you have to pass or fail because of somebody else's feelings or to get back at somebody or to get some attention. Ask for some help on this. *Keep schoolwork in a separate part of your head from your other problems.*

I would like to pass and get my diploma someday, but I hang out with some friends who brag about flunking out, not doing homework, and giving the teachers a hard time. What can I do?

You are in a tough spot. Everybody likes to be liked by their friends. If you are the leader of the group, you can take a strong stand and turn the group around. But if you are just one of the bunch, you are going to have to do some thinking.

First, ask a counselor to put you in some classes different from your friends. Get the teacher to change your seat in study hall so you can get some studying done there. If you get kept after school, do some catch-up work then.

Learn to do everything you can to keep your grades up without making a show of it. If you don't want to be seen carrying your books home, get your brother or sister to do it if they don't mind. Ask a friend to do it. Carry papers in your boots or inside your jacket. Try to stay on the edge of trouble, not in it.

Sooner or later you will have to decide what is important to you. If you have to break away to save yourself, you may be in for quite a battle. Remember this, though: A lot of people have broken away and been very glad they did. Do you really want not to be a ball player or a chemist or a furniture maker and be stuck in a boring job all your life because of the "friends" you hung out with when you were a teenager?

I really am bored, honest. If something interests me, I do okay, but that doesn't happen very often.

You probably don't do homework very often, either. A lot of really bright students get out of the habit of studying when they are in fourth or fifth grade because they can get by on their brains and a little bit of studying. Then when they get to junior high and high school, they don't really know how to make themselves sit down, get to work, and learn hard or boring stuff.

The older you get, the harder it is to get by on brains alone. It takes some real studying to learn some of the senior high course work. Yes, there will be boring work. It is part of everything you learn that is important.

If you really are super bright, you might be better off if you can get switched to classes or a school for the gifted and talented. You might find those classes more interesting. But your problem won't go away until you learn how to make yourself study and do the work required whether it is interesting or not. Try to find imaginative ways of sticking to a task. You may well work better if you team up with another student like yourself. You also might try doing some of your work on a computer. Be creative in doing projects. Find ways to make them more interesting to you by adding drawings or models or music to go with them.

I wouldn't mind school if it was just a few weeks a year, but it goes on and on and on— day after day, year after year. It just takes too long to get a diploma.

You are suffering from what some people call the problem of "instant gratification." You are not alone. We all have the problem to some degree.

What we mean by instant gratification is this: In these electronic times, a great many things in our lives come to us with the turn of a switch, the push of a button, or a wave of a hand. Just think, our grandparents did not have freezers or tape decks or TVs when they were young. Life moved much more slowly then, and people expected it to. Today, though, we expect to be able to get so many things so quickly, we haven't learned how to wait and take our time. Therefore, when it comes to learning, or getting over a bad injury, or watching someone suffer from a long illness, we find it hard to be patient, because we haven't had much practice at it.

We don't yet know how to stick a wire in your head and program you for all you need to know in life. That day will probably never come. That is why you have to go to school for so many years.

Grandmother or Grandfather may have loved school and can't understand why you don't. For them going to school *kept* them from being bored. They had the same feelings you do, but it is hard for them to see it your way. Without television or video tapes, the best way they could learn about all the interesting things in the world was through books and listening to older people talk. They may not be able to see things your way, but try to see things their way. Meantime, just keep on going to school. You've come such a long way toward getting your diploma already. It won't be much longer!

School is bad. Teachers are worse. They are always picking on me. Why won't they leave me alone?

If you *really* want to know, ask some of your friends. Most likely, you know in your heart what the problems are already. Getting along with teachers is sometimes just a matter of knowing how to play the game. Remember these points if you want to get along with teachers.

- *Teachers are human, too—even the meanest of them. They will like you better if you smile when you talk to them. They will treat you better if you act polite and speak softly. Do not use loud, rough language like you might use with your friends. Be a smart salesperson. If you can get the teacher to feel you are not the enemy, you will get along much better. Some teachers may actually be afraid of you. Don't use that to get your way.*

In the long run it will work against your passing the course.

- Teachers like to teach. They like to see students pass. They will help you, but they won't do the work for you. Try to learn the difference.
- Be slow to decide that a teacher really hates you or has something against you personally. Many very good teachers may give you a hard time to get your best work from you because they think you are worth fighting for. You often learn the most from "mean" teachers.
- If you think you are dealing with a real case of prejudice—if you think your teacher hates you because of your race or nationality—be sure to report it to the school principal or to someone higher up. A real case of prejudice is one where the teacher calls you names or makes racial, religious, or other slurs. If this happens, deal in

facts—not your feelings. Report exactly what happened. Don't blow up in class. Keep your cool and you can stop a bad situation from happening again. Get a change, not revenge—no matter how much you want to.

- *Never strike a teacher. No matter what your reason, you will always get in trouble doing that. If you have a teacher you really can't get along with, ask to be transferred to another class. If you can't get a transfer, ask another teacher you can trust to help you work out a plan for getting along. Don't just keep on having an angry time with the teacher. Take responsibility for working out a plan to get along better.*

All this stuff you are saying is pretty interesting, but I've made up my mind. I really don't want to go to the trouble to study hard. I am just not going to do it.

Then make up your mind also that you probably won't graduate. It takes hard work to pay the rent, buy food, get an education. Wise people learn not to fight hard work, but to do it as cheerfully as they can.

Hard work is like jogging or bike riding. At first it is pure pain to push yourself to run farther or bike faster. But if you keep on doing it, the pain lessens and the satisfaction increases. Soon, you really miss the jogging or biking if you don't get to do it.

We won't say that you will get to a point where you love doing schoolwork, but you can get to a point where you don't mind it so much and you get a lot of satisfaction out of doing pretty fair in your studies. Best of all, you will feel better about yourself. You won't feel like a loser all the time.

Okay. Suppose I decide to really try to stay in school. What do I need to do first?

As we said before, your goal is to study smarter—not longer. Make your study time pay off! What is important is that *you* figure out a plan that is best for you. You know where you need help or need a push from somebody. You decide how to do it, then take action. It will take time to get the hang of it, and you will not always do it right. The important thing is for you to decide where you are going and how you will get there. Then you can be sure you will make it.

Here are some ways you could go about learning to quit hating school (and yourself):

1. *Aim for making one grade higher than you have been making in your three most important classes.*

2. *Use this book to help you do homework faster, study more effectively, and make better grades on tests.*

3. *Join one new school club or make one new friend at school— student, teacher, or worker around the school. Get to know this person well enough that you will be glad to see them every day. Make a point of seeing this person daily—even just to say hello. It makes school a friendlier place.*

4. *Be sure you know the school rules. Do not cut the first day of a new class, the day before a test, or the test day. The more days you go to class, the better your grades are likely to be. Try never to cut your hardest class. Teachers find it hard to fail somebody who comes every day.*

5. *Speak up in class discussions. Try to find something interesting to say at least once a week.*

6. *Remember your manners when you talk to teachers or principals.*

7. *Protect yourself. If you have any cuts, detentions, sus-*

pensions, etc., keep a record of them. Then if disagreements ever occur over whether you have lost credit for too many cuts, you have something to back your claims.

8. Take charge of your school life. You make the big decisions. Don't blame others. It is your choice whether you graduate. Don't let others tell you you can't do it. You can.

2
HOMEWORK
MADE EASIER

Does the very thought of homework put a knot in your stomach? Homework is one of the biggest problems with school for a lot of people. Some people forget to do it, others have problems doing it, and still others have problems remembering to take it in to school.

I hate homework. I think teachers give it just to be mean.

Once in a while teachers give homework for punishment, but most teachers don't. Don't forget, teachers have to work nights to grade the homework they give you, so it's work for them, too. This means that they have to have a pretty good reason for giving you homework or they wouldn't do it.

Understanding the reason behind a teacher's giving you homework will make it easier for you to decide how much to do and when to do it.

A few teachers give homework only because they are told they have to. You can spot these teachers easily. The homework isn't very hard, isn't always collected, and may not be graded. Do that homework last unless you have some problem understanding the work.

Some teachers give homework to help them judge whether you understand the work. Many math teachers explain problems in class and then ask you to do some problems like those at home. It is smart to do at least some of each kind of problem. That way you can find out if you really did understand. Math homework is very important because each year builds on what you learned the year before. If you miss out and don't understand one part, it can give you trouble.

Some teachers give homework that covers books or papers that won't be covered in class, but that you may be tested on. You better do enough of that homework to understand it.

Some teachers give outside projects—reports, research papers, oral presentations, etc.—that make up a big part of your grade. This is very important homework because you have to plan how to do it and get it in on time. See the chapter in this book on report writing to help you make the plan you need and stick to it.

Homework really gets me down. I mean to do it, but I just can't seem to get started.

Join the club. When we sit down to write, we often find that we keep getting up to get something to eat or to sharpen pencils. Then we have to make a phone call or maybe watch a TV show we've been waiting for. Pretty soon it's time to feed the cat and we haven't gotten anything done. If anybody asks, we say, "Yeah, I worked awhile this afternoon, but I didn't get as far as I wanted to. I know now what I need to do tomorrow."

Who are we trying to fool? We didn't work a lick. The next day, of course, we're even further behind and more discouraged.

You, too, huh? So how do you ever get started?

You get started by realizing that you have a bad habit. The best way to break it is to do it by little stages.

For example, start by planning to work only fifteen minutes on your math homework. Sit down and start. Don't eat, answer the phone, or get off your chair. Just dig in for fifteen minutes. Then get up and call it a day. You will feel a lot better about yourself when you see you can really do it. Try it for a day or two.

As you get used to working hard for fifteen minutes, add five minutes. Pretty soon you can work half an hour, take a break, and go back to work for another half hour. Honest, it really works.

I know this kid in school who runs home every day to do his homework. He says he enjoys it. Is he lying?

He may be telling the truth. Some people like to read and study. Others like to get good grades because it makes them feel good about themselves. Others study to get into a career or a college. Some study because they are lonesome and haven't

anything else to do. Some want to make their mom or dad happy. Others are jealous and want to do better than a brother or sister. Some people like a teacher a lot and want to do well in that class.

There are good and bad reasons for studying. Most people who pass have a combination of reasons. Why do *you* want to study—or not want to study? Your answer can help you know how much studying you need to do and what you will get out of your education.

When should I study? Mom wants me to study as soon as I get home.

Sit down with your mom and work out a plan that lets you do homework at a time you are at your best. Everybody has a time of day or night when they concentrate better. Yours might be late afternoon or even six o'clock in the morning. Once you pick a time, stick to it. Let people know that is your time and they should leave you alone. If you don't use that time for watching TV or talking on the phone, they will know you are serious.

Where can I study? Trying to do homework at my house is impossible.

People find all kinds of places to study. What you want to look for is a place where you can be comfortable, have your books, and can work without people bothering you. Here are some places you might try:

Your aunt's house. At your church (ask the minister). The library (a great place). The recreation center building (ask the leader). The doughnut shop (always buy something). A friend's house (is it okay with his folks?). Don't forget study hall and working at school in a favorite teacher's classroom.

Do not study on the job unless you have the kind of job where the boss says you may. When you are on the job, the job comes first.

Glad you brought up the job. I'm really beat when I get home from my job—too tired to do homework. Why can't my teachers understand that?

They do understand. They understand that you have made a choice of job over school. If you want to work, you must plan to work only in the hours you don't need for school or homework. If you *have* to work, take fewer classes. It may

take you longer to graduate, but that way you can do a good job both at school and at work.

If you spend all your time on the job and don't do homework, you may flunk out. Take a hard look at what you are doing to yourself. Most people out of their teens find it a lot easier to make higher wages and to get good jobs if they have high school degrees. They also find it is expensive to try to go back and get a high school degree later in life when they have to take time off from work and pay for classes. This may be the only time in your life when you can get a free education.

How can I get people to quit trying to make me do my homework?

The easiest way is to do your homework! But we don't think that is what you are asking. The best way is to decide for yourself that you are really in charge of your school life. After all, no one can *make* you do your homework. They can try to make you wish you had done it, but that's all. *You are the only person who decides whether you will do your homework.*

This means there is no point in blaming your teacher for giving you too much work, or your parents for fussing at you about chores, or your friends for trying to get you to go to a show instead of studying. You choose. Your work is your responsibility and yours alone—pass or fail.

This doesn't mean that what you do won't affect other people. Teachers feel sad when students fail and happy when they pass. Parents are the same. But that is their business. You hurt yourself most of all when you choose to let school be a road to failure instead of success.

When you show people that you are taking charge of your life in a responsible way, they will quit bugging you.

I like to flop out on my bed and turn on the TV while I do my homework. What do you say about that?

There are times this is okay if you just have the TV on for background noise. You can probably do simple questions in a workbook. For serious study, though, you better get rid of the TV.

As for flopping out on the bed, there are two ways of looking at it. Everyone agrees that you can write more neatly and clearly sitting at a desk. For the final paper in English, you will need to sit at a desk to do it right. Some people also concentrate better if they sit at a table and sit up straight. It seems to keep their minds on what they are doing.

On the other hand, some people say they have to be able to move around and flop about to study. Some people say they can concentrate better if they are wiggling their feet or swinging their arms. Still others say they can think their best while stretched out on a bed or on the floor. Since you can't very well do any of these things at school, you need to be able to study sitting down at least some of the time. However, if you do find that you need to be on the move while you study, you may be doing what is best for you. Try it both ways and see.

Lots of times I don't finish all my homework, so I just don't turn any of it in. There's no point in it.

Don't be too sure. A zero won't help you at all, but if the teacher gives you even a few points, you will be further ahead.

Suppose you have ten assignments to do in the next grading period. You do all but two of them. On the papers you turn in you get a couple of 75s, a 70, and five 65s. Looks like you will pass, right? *Wrong.* If you average in the two zero grades for the papers you didn't turn in, your average drops to 54. But if you had turned in even a little bit of homework those two days, you might have gotten an additional 50 and a 30. If you average those two grades in, that would give you enough to pass.

Don't overlook the importance of even one or two grades. Your work may be far from perfect, but it may be close enough to keep you in the race.

Another reason for turning in even a line or two of homework is that it lets the teacher know you remembered and gave some effort. If you don't finish work because you don't

understand it, this will also let the teacher know you need some extra help.

What should I do when I get behind in my homework? Sometimes I get sick and don't do any. Sometimes I just don't do any for a week or two. Then I quit trying because I'm going to flunk anyway.

If you miss one or two days' homework or even a week's, try to do the newest homework first and gradually catch up on the back work as you go along. If you do the newest first, you can understand what is going on in class better.

In math, you may have to plan on going to the teacher during lunch or after school or getting an older brother or sister to help you catch up. You can't skip over back work in math. You have to take it one step at a time.

But suppose you have been a total goof-off. Four or five weeks have passed and you have done hardly any homework. You have gotten by in class on your brains and from listening. Suddenly it hits you that you are going to fail. Are you? Not necessarily.

Go to the teacher and say that you are sure you can never catch up on all the back work, but that you really want to pass. Ask the teacher to lay out for you the smallest amount of homework you could do that would bring you up to a passing grade. If you are sincere, many teachers will give you a very big break that one time and ask you to do only a part of the back work. Most teachers want to help a student to pass and will try to give you a fair chance.

My buddy says that smoking a little pot will help me concentrate when I do my homework. Is that possible?

Yes, it is "possible." It is also "possible" to run across a superhighway in the middle of heavy truck traffic going sixty miles an hour. But there are some problems with both.

You might get away with either a time or two, but in the long run you will get hurt.

We called the National Organization for Reform of Marijuana Laws (N.O.R.M.L.) in Washington, D.C., and asked them your question. They are the group that held the "smoke-ins" in the capital and believe that pot should be declared legal.

The man who answered my question spoke very strongly. He said, "We believe that growing up should be drug-free. That includes all the drugs—alcohol, pot, PCP, cocaine, LSD, pills, and so on." He went on to say, "I wish I hadn't started smoking pot as early as I did. I wish I hadn't skipped school so much. Smoking pot in high school caused me a lot of problems."

I get so bored with homework. After school I want to be with my friends. How can I work that out?

How about some buddy-study? Pick a friend who is willing to put in some time studying with you. Go someplace quiet two or three afternoons a week and put in an hour or two of study time together. It makes the studying go faster because you can help each other. You will still have to put in some study time on your own, probably, but working together can make study time more fun.

Studying with your steady might be a little trickier. Unless you can keep your mind on your books, don't try it. You are only fooling yourself.

My dad tries to help me with my homework, but he really gets in my way. How can I get him to lay off?

Get him to send for a little book called *How to Help Your Children Achieve in School*. It costs $3.75, and you get it by writing to Consumer Information Center, Dept. 109M, Pueblo, CO 81009. That will help him see how to help you and when he should leave you alone.

I don't know why Dad picks on me about my homework so much.

Does it ever sound like this at your house?

DAD: **Any homework?**

YOU: **Nope, did it all in school.**

DAD: **Your English teacher called and said you have a paper to do.**

YOU: **Oh, that. I can't do it. I left it in my locker.**

DAD: **She read me the assignment. Here it is.**

YOU: **Okay, okay, I was going to do it. I'd just forgotten it.**

DAD: Here's the assignment. Go do it *now*.
YOU: Dad, I can't. Mom told me to clean my room. I'll do it after dinner, honest.
DAD: You better. I don't want any more calls about you.
YOU: Relax, Dad. I've got everything under control.

You bet your boots, you've got everything under control. You are controlling your parents by stringing them along about your homework. Why do you do it?

Is it possible that by not doing your homework you keep them paying attention to you when you are feeling sort of neglected now that you are a teenager? Or are you mad at them and you know this is a way to bug them? Or are you covering up some other feeling?

Don't act like a little kid. In the long run you could be the one who flunks out of school and doesn't graduate. You are the one who will be hurt the most. There are better ways to deal with feelings.

Mom says I don't get enough sleep. I must admit I am sort of blah in class some days, but it's because the class is so boring.

Research shows that if you don't get enough good, rested sleep, your whole body will be unable to do its best. Why do you think pro football players have bed checks and have to go to bed at a reasonable hour? The coaches know they have to be rested to do well.

People do vary in the amount of sleep they need, but most people can't get by on four or five hours a night. Some people get that little because they stay up and watch late night TV. If you do that, there is no way you won't feel blah in class. The most exciting class in the world is going to go right over your head if you are let down from lack of sleep. It is very hard to concentrate on difficult ideas if you are sleepy and tired. In fact, repeated days of lack of sleep can begin to do your body real harm.

I've tried, but I just can't learn.

No way. You were born liking to learn. Learning is as natural as eating. Think of all the things you know now that you didn't know when you were in first grade. The problem comes when someone tells you what to learn and you don't particularly want to learn it. The key to learning is being willing to try.

My math teacher says my paper is always the messiest one that's turned in. I never get the problems right anyway. Why should I bother trying?

Maybe the two problems are related. The lines on regular notebook paper help you write neatly across a page, but they don't help you do math neatly. Turn your paper on the side so that the lines form columns. You'll find that your math problems are easier to keep in their correct columns and will certainly be neater. Because you can keep each column in line, you will probably get more problems correct.

You might also try doing your math homework on graph paper.

$$
\begin{array}{ccc}
4 & 2 & 2 \\
  & x & 2 \\
\hline
8 & 4 & 4
\end{array}
$$

Are there some other studying tips that would help me do my homework better?

Yes, there are a couple of things that can help. Research shows that long hours of watching TV make it almost impossible for some people to actively read and study afterwards. There is a kind of hypnosis in TV that leaves you groggy and sleepy. You know yourself you sometimes end up being plugged into the screen for a couple of hours when you only meant to watch one show.

TV is a hard habit to break. The people who buy ad time on TV count on keeping you hooked. Just remember, when you watch hour after hour of TV you are letting someone else control what you do with your time. Is that what you really want?

Another thing you might check out. Too much candy and soft drinks can leave you feeling blue and blah when the buzz wears off from the first jolt of sugar. You might be better off with a piece of fruit or a peanut butter sandwich. What you eat can make a difference when you try to put in a couple of hours studying.

Learn to write down the big homework assignments—like research papers and book reports—on a calendar in your room. If you see the date on your calendar getting closer and closer, it is easier to keep on reading the book or writing the paper.

Just think of homework as something you do every day like combing your hair. The less you fight it, the easier it will be.

Sometimes I'm so tense and nervous, I just can't study. How can I relax?

If you have something worrying you, you may find it hard to stop worrying and start studying, but you can do it.

First, be sure you have done all you can to solve the problem for the time being. Then do some relaxation exercises. Yelling and cursing and pounding with your fists won't make problems go away. Those things just make you more tense. Crying can help. Some scientists believe that a good, quiet cry helps get rid of some of the body chemicals that make you tense.

Try this. Sit in a comfortable chair. Close your eyes and try to picture in your mind some quiet place where you were once very happy. See yourself walking around in that place. Look at all the things around you. Remember how good it felt. Were there flowers to sniff or bread baking or some other good smell? Perhaps there was music that you can hear again in your imagination. Finally, as you walk around you see a light coming through a door. Open the door and walk through. When you walk through, open your eyes.

If you have not been interrupted during this exercise, you will probably find that you now feel relaxed and rested. Go get something to drink and then try your studies.

I feel better already. I might even do my homework.

Good for you. Remember, the more often you do the homework, the easier it will get and the better you will feel about yourself. You won't always be having to dodge teachers and parents. You can look them in the eye, grin, and say, "I did it." And when they don't believe you, you can pull out the proof.

3
READING BETTER AND FASTER

When most people think about school, they think of readin', writin', and 'rithmetic, just as the old song says. If you hate school, the chances are that you associate reading with everything bad about school and hate it, too. Or at least you hate reading the kinds of things teachers tell you to read.

Why do I have more trouble with reading now than I did when I was younger?

In the early days you usually read stories. Stories are called *narrative* writing. They are fun to read and one thing that happens leads to another. They are also about people and things in your own life or things you might like to do.

Now you are asked to read about facts and ideas. This is called *expository* writing. This is harder to read because there are lots of ideas and words that are new to you and there is no story line to follow. It is easy to feel like you are lost in a big confusing city with no map.

What can I do that will help me understand better when I read confusing books?

You need to draw your own map as you go along so you won't get lost—just like you would do if you were going to explore a new part of town. If you go exploring, you watch very carefully what kinds of stores you pass and how many blocks you go. Even if you don't draw it on paper, you make a sort of mental map so you can find your way back home.

Reading expository materials is done the same way. As you read along, try to figure out where the writer is trying to take you. It may help to make some notes on paper as you go along to give you a map to follow. Look out for words and ideas that you already know. You have stored lots of old ideas in your mind over the years, and you can remember them when you try. Put new ideas together with old ones so the new ones make more sense to you. For example, if you read about a sickness called elephantiasis, you already know that an elephant is big. You guess that a person with elephantiasis swells up. You read on and discover that indeed a person with that sickness swells in the arms and legs. Now you have a new word, and you can remember it.

Why do I read whole pages and then it will hit me that I didn't understand a word of it?

You are not *monitoring* yourself. Good readers check themselves every paragraph or so to be sure they understand what they are reading. Ask yourself, "What did the writer mean by that?" If you don't know, then go back and find out where you stopped understanding.

You have two jobs in understanding new material. First, you need to learn the meaning of words that are new to you (and learn to pronounce them so you can use them). Second, you have to understand the new word well enough to store it and the ideas it stands for in your mind. If you have trouble remembering new words, see the chapter in this book on remembering.

I don't know why the teacher makes such a big deal over word lists. I usually know most of them already.

A teacher gives a word list to help you understand what you are reading. The words are chosen because they are key words that need your special attention. You will be reading them, hearing them, writing them, and perhaps be tested on them.

Watch out! Sometimes you run across a word you think you know, but suddenly what you are reading doesn't make any sense. This happens more and more as you read harder books because many words have different meanings even though they are spelled exactly the same way. For example, the word "prime" has different meanings depending on whether it is used in math (*prime* numbers), social studies (*prime* interest rate), auto mechanics (*prime* a motor), or home economics (*prime* beef).

It's important to remember that there are multiple meanings of words. If the teacher asks you to take a word list home, look up the words, and write down the definitions. Unless the teacher tells you otherwise, don't just write down

the first definition following the word; read all the definitions and see which one makes sense in the subject you are studying.

A dictionary is a good friend to have. The more you use it, the better you will understand how it can help you in spelling and writing and understanding what you study. If you have to get up from where you are studying and go to another room to find the dictionary to look something up, you won't be likely to use the dictionary very often. You really need one of your own that you can keep close to where you study. Dictionaries are very different; some are hard to use, others easy. Look at several of them to find the kind that works best for you. If you have reading problems that make it hard for you to find words in the dictionary, look for one of the big-print dictionaries with fewer words. (Ignore the fact they are called beginner books—you don't need to worry about that, you have school to worry about!) For the words not in your dictionary, you may need to ask someone to tell you the meaning of words or help you look them up in a harder dictionary. However, if you do this too often, you will probably find that people get tired of helping you.

Many people keep a list of new words they learn in each course. Some people put the new words on cards, some put them in a notebook, and some (who learn better by listening than looking) put them on their tape recorders. When it comes time to study for a test, you can just pull out your list (or put on your earphones) and review.

There's no doubt about it—the more words you learn, the easier it is to read hard books.

I don't know why I hate to read, but I just do.

There could be lots of reasons why you don't like to read. You may have had a hard time learning to read, so other people made fun of you. You may have been punished by being made to read, or you may have been put under a lot of pressure to read before you were ready. If you don't like to read because you read slowly or don't understand what you read, you would probably enjoy reading more if you got some special reading teacher to help.

Don't confuse not liking to read or not being able to read well with not being able to learn. You can learn by listening as well as by reading. Good listening can also make reading easier.

Do you mean using tapes?

Tapes can be useful, but the most important listening you do for school is the listening you do in class. If you really listen carefully, you will find that reading your textbook will be much easier, because most teachers will tell you in class the important points to focus on when you do read.

Listening to learn means that you really work at listening—you don't just sit in the back row chewing gum and watching the hockey players out on the field. Instead, you focus your eyes on the teacher—right between the teacher's eyes is a good spot. The teacher's facial expressions and hand movements often tell you when the teacher is talking about something important.

You will want to listen for words like "notice this," or "main idea," or "chief reason." Those words tell you to be sure to remember certain points; they also tell you that this is a good time to take some notes. Some people use tape re-

corders in class, but there is a big problem with tapes. It takes you longer to review a tape of a class than to read over notes.

When it comes to reading novels and short stories, you may want to take advantage of all the tapes that are now on the market. Many libraries have tapes you can borrow at no cost. You can probably find some of the novels you have to read for school and you can also find books just for fun.

You can also tape your own books and stories. Offer to clean house for your grandmother while she reads to you and you tape her. That way you can go back over the tapes when you need to study for a test. If you don't have a grandmother, maybe somebody at a nursing home would like to read to you just to have your company. Don't knock it until you try it.

Tapes are especially useful because you can listen to them in the car or at night in bed or while you jog. You can tape test material you want to learn and you can tape spelling words, too.

Are there any shortcuts to reading?

One of the best ways is to talk to people who have already read whatever it is you need to read. If it is a novel, ask them to explain the plot. If it is a chapter of a textbook, ask them to explain the main ideas. Many teachers will be willing to do this if you ask them after school. Sometimes you can get someone who is a grade or two ahead of you to help you, too.

Another shortcut that helps is to read a summary of a novel *before* you read the book itself. Summaries let you know what to look for and what the main ideas are. You can find these summaries in both new and used book stores. But don't fool yourself—you can't pass a test on a novel just by reading the summary.

I read everything very slowly, but I still don't understand a lot of what I read.

Reading slowly isn't always the best way. In fact, sometimes if you read too slowly, you lose the point the author is making because you're paying attention to the words—not the ideas.

Speed in reading is like speed in driving a car—how fast you go depends on the situation. In a car sometimes you go slowly; for example, when you're in traffic or when you're looking for a certain place and don't know where it is. Other times, when you are on a long trip, you go very fast along the highway.

Reading speed is the same. If you are reading a <u>recipe or directions</u> on how to put something together, you'll go very slowly so that you will not miss any of the details. <u>You read every word.</u> If you are reading a <u>novel</u> you really enjoy, you may want to read it slowly, too, but often, if you are reading a novel, you want to go very quickly. You simply want to get to the end of it. <u>You read important words and key phrases, not every little word.</u>

How do you read just key words and phrases?

To do that you have to force yourself to skip over unimportant words and pay attention to the words that give you the main idea.

Look at the last paragraph in the answer to the last ques-

HOW TO READ KEY WORDS!

tion, the one about reading speed. Notice that some words are underlined. As you read, let your eyes light mainly on the underlined words and skim over the others. Just by looking at those underlined words you can get the sense of the paragraph without reading it word for word.

Your eyes should look for important words that carry the meaning of what you are reading. Often these are the nouns and the verbs. Skim over the rest of the words. Remember, not all words require an equal amount of your attention for you to get the general idea. If you learn to do this, your understanding will improve, too, since you won't be slowed down by reading w-o-r-d-b-y-w-o-r-d.

Is that what the teacher means by skimming and scanning?

Basically, yes. When you *skim* a page, you try to get the general idea by reading just the important words and phrases. When you *scan* a page you are doing the same thing, but you are looking for a particular piece of information.

Scanning works like this. Suppose a couple of weeks from now you need to answer the question, "How can I read a long novel? I read so slowly." You would check the index or flip through this book until you came to this chapter. Then you would glance at all the questions in this chapter until you came to the one that had the words "I read everything slowly." Next you would glance at each paragraph until you came to one that had the word "novel" in it. You would slow down there and look for the answer to your question. Looking for a friend's name in a telephone book is another example of scanning. You don't read every name; you just glance at column after column until you find one that has names beginning with the same letters as your friend's name. Only then do you slow down and start reading name by name.

I try, but I have trouble skimming and scanning.

One reason you may have trouble skimming and scanning is because you are unconsciously saying every word to yourself. This is called "vocalizing" (or "subvocalizing," if you do it way down in your throat). You can tell if you vocalize by resting your hands gently on the side of your throat while you read some easy materials. You will feel the vibrations.

Vocalizing slows down your reading considerably. It keeps

HOW TO OVERCOME VOCALIZING
OR
HAVE FUN SPEEDING UP YOUR READING RATE!

you reading only as fast as you can speak—a rate much slower than that at which your eyes can move.

The cure is simple—chew gum when you read. Talking and chewing at the same time are impossible. It also helps just to know that you are vocalizing and that it slows you down.

Also, the more you know about a topic, the easier it is to use key words and phrases. If you don't know much about a topic, you have to slow down and read more of the words until you begin to understand what you are reading.

Suppose I read fast but don't remember a thing I read? What do I do when that happens?

Don't keep turning the pages. Stop reading, figure out what your problem is, and take fix-it steps.

Ask yourself if the problem is not knowing enough about what you are reading. You may have to go back and read something easier to give you the background information that you need.

Do you have something more important on your mind? Talk to someone about it and then go back to studying.

Are you having trouble concentrating? Slow down and take notes.

The answer may lie in just slowing down and not trying to read a week's work in fifteen minutes! Be honest with yourself. Don't say, "I've done all my homework—I read all forty-eight pages," when you know you didn't grasp a single idea in what you read.

Sometimes when I'm reading, I find myself reading the same lines over and over.

The fact that you recognize that you are reading lines several times is a good start—you are beginning to monitor yourself. Here are some things to try that may help.

Force your eyes to move ahead. Promise yourself if you concentrate hard on what you are reading for fifteen minutes you will reward yourself with a ten-minute break to do what you like. Fifteen minutes of concentrated reading is more valuable than one hour of time in which your mind wanders and you keep thinking how sorry you feel for yourself.

If you have trouble focusing your attention for even fifteen minutes, reading out loud can help you concentrate on the material. Reading out loud is especially helpful if the material is difficult and if you stop often to ask yourself if you understand what you are reading.

Mom nags me all the time about reading more. I can read okay and I'm not going to forget how.

In a way you are right. Reading is a skill you won't forget easily. But in a way your mom is right, because, as with any other skill, if you stop doing it for a while you are going to be rusty when you go back to it. If you keep on reading, you keep on learning. The more you know, the faster you can read and the more you can understand of what you do read.

I have a job and I can't spend a lot of time reading. What's the best way to study a chapter of a textbook for homework?

Let us tell you the *worst* way first. That's to start at the beginning of the chapter and read right through, word by word by word, to the end. You'll end up lost in a maze of words.

Your goal is to pick out the main ideas first. *Then* go back and learn the details.

First read the chapter summary several times, if there is one, and then read what is under the pictures. Read the headings and subheads, and what's set off in special type. Then check yourself. Can you explain the most important ideas in the chapter?

You may need to know all the important ideas plus lots of details to get an A on a quiz, but just knowing the important ideas will often get you at least a passing grade.

By going for the main ideas you will know a lot more than if you try to force yourself to wade through the entire chapter, reading every single word as fast as you can.

How can I read better without being in some special class?

A lot of people say that the best way to learn to read better is to read, read, read. Exercises and drills and worksheets won't help if you don't actually pick things up and read them. The best way is to pick something that *really* interests you— it may be about off-road vehicles, or TV actors, or old cookbooks. Whatever it is, go to yard sales or used-book stores or library sales and start collecting every book and magazine you can find on the subject. Sooner than you think, you will be reading better and you will be a kind of expert on that subject. You may even find yourself saying, "The other day I was reading that . . ." surprising yourself at what you know. Reading can make you feel special.

If you are still having trouble reading, but you don't want to be in a special education class, hire a reading teacher to work with you. If you don't have the money, swap mowing lawns or washing the dog or cleaning the basement in exchange. A good reading teacher can help you read faster and more easily.

Don't let your feeling about schoolwork spoil the fun of reading. Read and enjoy!

4
HOW TO REMEMBER

Do you have trouble remembering to do your homework or remembering what homework you are supposed to do? Worse, do you study and then find out that the next day you can't even remember what you studied?

Are you kidding? I forget my homework nearly every day. I sometimes forget things I really want to remember. Can I do anything about that?

Memory is a complex process. Even scientists don't know exactly how it works. We have some control over what we remember, but we don't control it entirely. People differ on how easily they remember different things. Remembering is also a skill, and all of us can improve memory by practicing and by knowing more about the conditions under which we are more likely to remember things.

Like what kind of conditions?

- *You tend to remember things that are* personally important. *You might forget to buy thumbtacks if your dad asked you to get them for his office, but you would probably remember to buy them if he told you he was going to use them to hang up a model you made.*
- *You tend to remember the first and last* items on a list. *If your aunt asked you to go to the store for eggs, milk, potatoes, oranges, sugar, and salt, you are more likely to remember the eggs and salt because they are first and last.*
- *You tend to remember something if it is* associated with *something you already know. Suppose you met a boy named Frank Wilson, who told you that his sister is Shirley Wilson in your class. You know Shirley pretty well, so you will probably remember Frank's name.*
- *You tend to remember things that are* repeated. *TV ads take advantage of this. The station will play a commercial over and over until you are sick of it, but you will remember the product.*
- *You tend to remember things that are* unusual. *Many rock stars dress in unusual outfits so you won't forget them.*
- *You tend to remember things that occur in a* pattern. *You would have little trouble remembering a locker combination that was 31-3-13.*

How can knowing that help me with remembering things for school?

Try to get interested in what you study. If you can see that learning fractions will be important in cooking or in repairing a motorcycle, you will find it easier to remember how to multiply fractions. Make your studies *personally important* whenever you can.

Study hard homework *first*. Repeat that poem you have to learn one *last* time just before going to bed.

Try to *associate* new words and ideas with old ones. You know the word "line." When you see the word "linear," you can remember that it has something to do with lines. You can

also use goofy associations to help you remember. To re-member that Frankfort is the capital of Kentucky, picture in your mind a Kentucky colonel eating a frankfort (hot dog) on a bun instead of fried chicken.

Learn a list of science terms by *repeating* them over and over. Say them to yourself over and over or write them down—whichever helps you remember better. By the way, it is better to space your repeating. Study the list now, then leave it for a while and come back to it later. Spaced learning is better and faster.

Use the *unusual* to help you remember things you need to do. Put big rubber bands around your sneakers at night so you will remember to pick up your history notebook and take it with you the next morning. Put one purple jelly bean in your lunch sack to remind you to go to your locker after lunch. Anything out of the ordinary will make you stop and remember.

If you are trying to learn a list, use *patterns.* Learn all the short words first, then all the long ones. Try singing lists. For example, you might sing the presidents of the United States to "Twinkle, Twinkle, Little Star." "Wash-ton, Adams, Jeff-son, Mad . . ."

Okay. I get the idea. I can try some of those. Do you know any others?

Sometimes it helps to know your learning style. By that we mean, do you learn better by seeing, hearing, or touching?

If you learn better by seeing things written down rather than having someone tell you, write things you want to learn on flash cards and keep flipping them. Draw little stick fig-ures to remind you of complicated ideas.

If you learn better by hearing things, get yourself a tape recorder. Spell words into the tape recorder and play them back to yourself. Read out loud.

If you learn better by getting the feel of things (if you are the kind of person who is good with your hands), write things you want to learn over and over until you get the "feel" of them. You may even make models of math problems to help you.

Most people learn by using a combination of senses, but other people learn mostly through one sense—seeing, hearing, or touching.

Sometimes I think I forget things because I have so many other things on my mind.

You are probably right. If you are going to remember something, you have to *want* to remember and you have to *concentrate* on it. You are absolutely wasting your time if you pick up your history book and flip pages while you think about something else. Put down the book and think through what is on your mind. Then go back and study with a clear head. You are only fooling yourself if you say you are studying when you are thinking about something else. Your mind will not remember any of the history material, and you won't be able to really think clearly about what *is* on your mind.

Before you start to study, ask yourself if you are ready to concentrate. If the answer is no, because you are thinking of last week's party and the one you are going to this weekend, you need to stop and remind yourself of why you are studying.

You are studying because *you* choose to study. If you don't study, you may fail the next test and *you* have decided you

don't want to fail the next test. As a way of helping you keep your mind on your work, put a check mark on a little scrap of paper every time you realize you have drifted off and started thinking about the party. Just being aware that you drift off will help you to concentrate.

My teacher is always telling me to write things down, clean out my notebook, bring a calendar to class. I just don't work that way. I wish my notebook was neater and I wish I didn't lose everything, but I'm always dropping my books or forgetting where I put them. If I do write stuff down on a calendar, I forget to look at the calendar. I'm hopeless.

Don't give up. As you grow older, you will get less clumsy and won't drop things as much. You will also find that using a calendar gets easier.

Meantime, let us tell you a secret. Some people are messy because they really want everything to be perfect, but since they can't keep things perfect, they don't try at all. Could that be your problem? If so, try to settle for just doing okay, and make things easier on yourself. Don't hate yourself because you drop things or forget now and then. It is okay to be human. You won't have nearly as many problems if you quit hating yourself for being messy.

I can see how it would help me if I kept track of things, but if I carry that little calendar around that my folks gave me, my friends would laugh me out of school.

Good point. If you are not comfortable with the system, you won't use it. You have to develop your own system that fits with your life-style and your personality.

If you have access to a computer with graphic possibilities, you can design your own system. You can make up calendars with only five days a week in them, or you can make up calendars with your friends' names all over them—whatever, just so long as you come up with something that you can enjoy looking at off and on every day.

If you don't have a computer, go to a card shop or a stationery store or an office supply place. There are more kinds of record-keeping systems than you can imagine. If someone tells you, "That is not designed to be a school calendar," thank them very much and take it anyway if it suits you.

A lot of high schoolers like to use the school's athletic

calendar for keeping track of things. Nobody laughs at keeping a folder of the dates for football and basketball games in a pants pocket.

It is your life. You need to know what is going to happen to you in school. Having your own way of keeping track will certainly save you from some ugly surprises and may provide you with some good ones!

Mom keeps saying that if I would just organize my notebook I'd do okay.

Some people need everything in neat order to work well. Others thrive happily in apparent (to others) disorder. It sounds as if you don't need everything to be perfect, but it also sounds like you aren't quite thriving. We think some kind of organization of your notebook would keep you from losing papers, but it has to be *your* organization. When we've suggested a three-ring binder to some teenagers, they have told us that binders like that aren't in style at their school. We had to compromise on something they didn't mind carrying. In each case the student came up with a different solution.

One girl elected to carry three half-inch binders in a backpack. She used one for homework, one for classwork and notes, and one for graded work for the marking period. One boy made a folder in wood shop that he liked to carry. Another girl arranged to carry the day's work in her jacket pocket and made arrangements with her teachers to keep paper and pencils in a hidden spot in the classrooms. Another boy carried a regular three-ring binder, but decorated it all over with his own designs.

Teachers have a right to expect you to bring the materials you need to class. You would expect a plumber who came to your house to fix a broken pipe to have tools, wouldn't you? So you are in charge of developing a system that works for you. That's how it is.

I never know what to remember. Sometimes I memorize a list of things and then find out the teacher only wanted me to read it. Other times I read something and find out the teacher wanted me to memorize it. I can't win.

You can win, but you have to learn to listen for the clues the teacher gives you and you have to be smart enough to get more information if the teacher isn't clear about what you are to do.

Listen very carefully to the words the teacher uses. If the teacher says to memorize, you know you are to learn it word for word. Listen for other words and phrases like "This will be on the test," or "Just be sure you understand this," or "Be able to tell me in your own words." Each of these phrases means something slightly different. Sometimes you may have to ask the teacher to be clearer about what you are to do, and most teachers will not mind if you ask. But be sure to say something like "Could you tell me one more time what you want us to do with this?" Don't whine, "Do I *have* to memorize this stuff?" That can make a teacher say, "Yes, you do," when the teacher didn't really start out to make you memorize it. Then all the rest of the class will really be mad at you.

But suppose the teacher says something like "Just learn everything in the chapter." Then what do you do? You can try going up to the teacher after class and asking him or her to help you figure out what is most important to study. If that doesn't or can't work, your next best bet is to talk to

someone in your class who usually makes pretty good grades—not necessarily the class brain, but somebody who is easy to talk to—and ask them what they study and how hard. It also helps to talk to a student who had the same teacher before. That person can tell you what kinds of tests the teacher usually gives. After one test, you will have a pretty good idea yourself about how hard you will have to study and can adjust your studying accordingly.

I try to take notes to help me study. I see everyone around me writing away, but nothing sounds important enough to write down. Besides, it's the same stuff that's in our book.

Remember what we said about repeating things helping you to remember? If you take notes, even on what is in the book, you are learning it. You are also reminding yourself what the teacher thinks is important (and likely to be on a test). Taking notes will help you pay attention and keep your mind from wandering, too.

Those reasons make sense. But what do I write down?

Be sure to write down anything the teacher says will be on the test, of course. Also write down anything the teacher introduces by saying, "Remember this," or "This is important," or "Don't forget." But don't put *everything* down. You will get lost. Try to put down just the main ideas. Imagine your mind as a filter. You collect what is going to remind you what the lesson is about that day.

Find a system that will help you make sense out of what you write down even a couple of months later. Some people use outlines. Others just keep running notes. Most people use abbreviations that make sense to them, even if they don't to anybody else. Still other people draw pictures and make diagrams. Try different things and see what works for you.

I can't listen and write at the same time. Even if I try, I can't write fast enough to take good notes in class.

Check with the teacher after school. Many teachers will let you look at their notes and let you copy them when you have time after class.

If that won't work, ask a friend to copy his or her notes for you by using NCR (no carbon required) paper. You can buy it at most office supply stores.

That sounds like I can forget about taking notes.

Not so fast. You will need to be able to take notes for your research papers. You will also find that it helps to take notes when you are reading some of your textbooks. Notes help you remember what you read, and are very useful when it comes time to study for a test. Keep practicing note-taking notes and you'll get faster.

What do you do when you forget things that you don't take notes on—like the name of a good friend or even my own phone number? That is really embarrassing.

We know! It happens to all of us—in school and out.

Here are some things you can try: Try to think of something else. It seems like the harder you try to remember something, the farther away it goes. Sometimes it helps to do something with your hands like untying and retying your sneakers. Another way is to picture yourself using the information in a different setting. If you can't remember your phone number, picture yourself calling the long distance operator and giving your area code. Sometimes that makes the number that follows pop into your head. Occasionally, nothing works for the moment, but in a little while the information just slips back in your head. Don't be too embarrassed. It happens to everybody now and then. People understand better than you think.

My folks are always getting after me because I forget to feed my dog or do something they asked me to do. They don't seem to be very understanding.

That may be a different kind of forgetting. Sometimes we forget because a part of us—deep down inside—*wants* to forget.

Suppose your mom asks you to go buy some cigarettes for her. You don't want her to smoke, but you plan to do as you were told. Somehow, though, you go all afternoon and never remember to buy her cigarettes.

Suppose you don't think your brother is doing his share of feeding the dog. You "forget" when it is your turn.

You are mad at your dad, and you know it makes him mad when you flunk a math test. You somehow "forget" to study and flunk the test the next day.

In each of these cases, you forget because a part of you wants to forget. By "forgetting" you stay in some kind of control of a situation. You kept your mom from smoking that night, you let your folks know there was a problem about feeding the dog, you got back at your dad—even though it hurt you.

There are better ways to handle each of these situations than by "forgetting." Talk to your mom and ask her not to send you for cigarettes because you love her and don't want to be part of her problem. Ask your brother and mom and dad to sit down and work out a plan for feeding the dog. Tell your dad why you are mad at him and try to get him to see what the problem is between you. When you "forget," you don't help solve the problem. Usually, you just make it worse.

I don't forget just a little. I forget a lot. I even forget important things that have happened to me. Am I nuts?

There are many reasons why you could have a serious memory loss. Brain injury from accidents or sickness of course causes memory problems. Very frightening or upsetting events may also cause memory problems. This is not uncommon. It doesn't mean you are nuts. If this kind of memory loss is troubling you, see your family doctor and talk to him or her about it. Don't keep on suffering.

We also know that if you are using drugs (including alcohol) you may have some memory loss. Drugs have different effects on different people. The very fact that drugs make you high or relaxed tells you that they have an effect on your brain. Sometimes this effect is hard to recognize in yourself. If you have been using drugs, ask a close friend or family member who doesn't use drugs if they have noticed any changes in you. If you are changing, be honest with yourself and seek help.

No one knows how to transplant brains, so take care of the one you have. How well you remember depends on how well your brain is functioning.

My friend says he uses memory tricks to keep from forgetting. What does he mean?

Maybe your friend is talking about mnemonics (pronounced ni-MAHN-iks). A mnemonic is just another kind of crazy association trick.

In one kind of mnemonic you use the first letter of each word in a list you want to remember. Suppose you have to learn this list for science class: kingdom, phylum, class, order, family, genus, species. Take the first letters of each word; k, p, c, o, f, g, s. Then make up a sentence like: Keep Pushing, Come On Fellows, Get Speed. That sentence is easy to remember and will help you say the list in order and will also remind you of the first letter of any one of the words you might forget. If you don't need to remember the words in order, make up a name using the first letters: F. G. Spock.

Another kind of mnemonic is called *visualizing*. You help yourself to remember something by making up a picture in your head. If you wanted to remember the last five presidents

of the United States, you might visualize Presidents Johnson and Nixon sitting in an old Ford truck at a drive-in eating Jimmy Carter's peanuts while watching an old Ronald Reagan movie.

Mnemonics help some people sometimes. Other people don't find them useful. Try and see for yourself.

Is it true that some people can remember without even trying?

It is true that some people seem to be able to remember a great many things almost without effort. They are said to have photographic memories. However, if you talk to a person with this skill, you will find that he or she uses a lot of the same tricks of association, repetition, patterning, visualizing, etc. Memory, like any other skill, is harder for some people and easier for others, but practice does help.

Remember, you can improve your memory. Don't forget it!

5

REPORT WRITING THAT WORKS

If you hate school, probably one of the things you most dislike is writing. We don't mean getting out a sheet of paper, putting your name and the date in the right-hand corner, and writing down the words needed to fill in worksheet blanks. We mean honest-to-goodness, come-up-with-a-topic, organize-your-thoughts, write-some-paragraphs-with-ideas-that-hang-together writing. It isn't easy for anyone. You can, though, do things that will make the process easier.

Well, I need some. My writing sounds so dumb that I put off doing it. I usually get a zero because I wait so long that it's useless to even turn in my paper.

Remember what we said about learning to read by reading? The same thing is true of writing. You need to plunge into writing without thinking about making each word perfect. Good writers don't *expect* their first copy to sound great. They put it aside, read it again later, and then rewrite. Just getting started is the important idea.

Boy, that sounds like work! I don't want to rewrite again and again.

It sounds worse than it is. How many times you rewrite is up to you, but plunge in and get started. "Plunge" is a good word, because writing is a lot like diving into a pool. It feels awful for a minute, but then you catch your breath and it gets better.

Think about the alternative. Spending time worrying about getting started doesn't help your mental state, doesn't get teachers and parents off your back, and doesn't get the job done. And making excuses doesn't make you feel good. You might be surprised at how easy writing is once you get started.

I don't know what to write about.

Pick something interesting to you. Pick a small topic.

I'm not interested in anything.

Do you like it when it snows up a real storm?

Sure. I get to stay home from school.

Okay, then write about snowstorms and why you like them.

That's dumb. The teacher won't like it, either.

Lots of our students say, "That's dumb," when we give them an idea, but they usually say that because what they really mean is "I don't want to do this report, and if I keep on calling everything dumb, maybe—somehow—I won't have to do the report."

You have to decide. Are you going to write the report or not? Don't waste your time messing with notes and books and stuff if you really don't plan to write it. You are just fooling yourself and wasting time when you might have fun doing something else. If it would make you feel good about yourself to get this report in on time, we can show you how to do it.

Okay, show me. I'll try to write it, but I have another problem. My teacher says to start with an outline and then write a topic sentence and then—on and on. It makes writing sound deadly.

Unfortunately, some teachers can make writing seem like that. Actually, once you get the hang of it, it is kind of fun to be able to write down what you think and know. You don't need to start with an outline, but you do need some way to collect your thoughts. Instead of an outline, try what some people call a *web.*

Put your topic, *Snowstorms,* at the top of the page. That's what your paragraph will be about. You could write books

about snowstorms, so you have to think about one part of that topic in which you are interested—that will be your title. Let's go with "Why I Like Snowstorms."

To write your first sentence, turn your title into a sentence. Since this first sentence introduces your topic—what you are going to write about—it is called the *topic sentence*. There are many sentences you could write, but let's go with "I like snowstorms because of the different things I do and the fun I have."

Write your topic sentence in the middle of your paper and draw an oval around it. What you have should look like this:

Topic: Snowstorms
Title: Why I Like Snowstorms

> **I like snowstorms because of the different things I do and the fun I have.**

Now think about what you need to say to support that topic sentence. Draw lines out from the oval and on those lines write down any details you can think of that support that first sentence. Remember, they *have* to be about the fun you have doing things that are not normally part of your daily life unless a snowstorm hits.

Here are some details you might want to describe: "not going to school," "eating a big breakfast," and "going outside." Two other things you might want to mention are "playing soccer in the snow" and "earning money shoveling driveways." Since these two are activities that you do outside, don't put them on separate lines from the oval; tie them to the line "going outside."

You want to mention the pancakes you love. Since they are a part of the "big breakfast," tie them to that line. Here's what your paper should look like now:

Topic: Snowstorms
Title: Why I Like Snowstorms

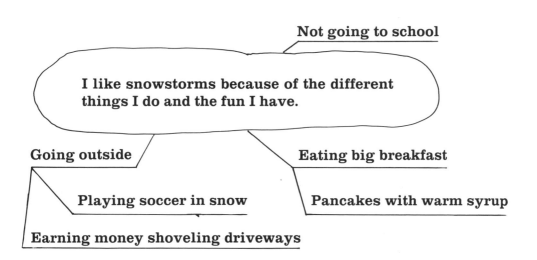

Look at what you have done. You've organized in a rather painless way what you're going to write about. You haven't gotten bogged down in a formal outline. (If your teacher insists, you can turn your web into an outline by following outline form.)

Your paper will practically write itself now. As you use each item on the web, picking in any order you want, cross it off. Then add a last sentence in which you basically repeat your first sentence, but say it in a slightly different way. Here's what you might turn in.

Why I Like Snowstorms

I like snowstorms because of the different things I do and the fun I have the next day. Waking up early and hearing on the news that there is no school is great. I always have a big breakfast. My brother and I fix pancakes and Mom warms maple syrup to go with them. Then I go outside to meet my friends. We walk around the neighborhood and make some money by shoveling out driveways. After lunch we play soccer in the snow. Snowstorms are great because of the fun I have afterwards.

Let's be realistic. This paragraph is not going to win you a writing award. Still, it is a good solid paragraph in which every sentence sticks to the topic. Writing a paper this way will get writing assignments done as quickly and painlessly as possible.

If you want to make it better, then you will need to rewrite it. You could add other examples, and use more vivid, exciting action words. It all depends on how good you want to make it.

That looks okay to me for one or two paragraphs, but I have a research paper due in three weeks!

Then you need to get started right away.

Has your teacher approved your topic? Teachers like a topic that is broad enough for you to find information easily, but narrow enough that you can stay focused on that subject.

Once your topic is approved, head for the nearest library and ask the librarian for help in locating material on your topic. An encyclopedia usually gives you an overview of your subject, and it can provide the framework for your paper, so you might want to start with that. Many teachers will allow you to use only one.

Besides books and magazines, you can also use interviews. Older people often like to be interviewed and can give you good ideas and information, so don't overlook your own grandmother or grandfather.

As you gather information, make notes *in your own words.* Teachers are experts at spotting material that's been copied and turned in as a student's own, and they don't view this kindly. Using your own words from the beginning will avoid this problem. Take notes on cards or in a notebook—however you work best.

How do I go about writing it once I have the notes?

Writing a research paper is the same process as writing that paragraph on "Why I Like Snowstorms," except that you go to the library for facts about snowstorms. Your paper will be a series of webs, each of which you'll turn into a para-

graph. Use a short paragraph at the beginning that introduces your subject and tells what you're going to write about.
If you used snowstorms as the subject of your research paper,
the introductory paragraph might look like this:

**Snowstorms, or blizzards, cause a lot of trouble in the
winter. This paper will talk about why we have snowstorms, what happens when we have one, and how
weather forecasters can tell when a snowstorm is on the
way.**

Then write a page or two on each one of those things you
said the paper would talk about—again using a web for each
topic to figure out what to say.

Don't forget to write an ending paragraph that ties everything together by summarizing what you wrote. Here's an example:

> **Since there will always be times in the winter when cold air and warm air meet, we will always have a risk of snowstorms. Even though a snowstorm can cause many problems, we have seen that weather forecasters are able to predict them better now.**

Suppose I do write the paper. I'm never sure I have done it right.

Most teachers are flattered if you ask for help. Your teacher will probably be pleased to read over your paper and may even help you correct your spelling and punctuation while doing so. English teachers especially are unable to resist changing incorrect commas!

That would help. I get really confused about where commas and periods go.

We're not going to give you the rules on punctuation here. You can easily find a grammar book to do that. There are some other ways around your problem. Try these:

- *We just mentioned having a teacher help you. If that doesn't work, read out loud what you have written. Put in a comma wherever you take a breath. Put in a period wherever you come to a full stop. If you find yourself stumbling over what you're reading, you probably have a punctuation problem at that point.*
- *Another way around your problem is to pay someone to read your paper and help you with spelling and punc-*

tuation. You might even want to hire a typist to both type and proofread. If you do, be honest with the teacher about having hired someone. Read it over yourself, anyway, as you are responsible for any errors. You might not have to pay in money. Maybe you can trade an oil change for help from a student who is good in English. Be creative in exchanging your talents for help you need.

Writing a long paper is too much for me, even though I can take notes and know in my mind what I want to say.

There are a couple of things you can do. If you talk better than you write, dictate your paper into a tape recorder and copy it down when you play the tape back. You could pay somebody to copy it for you, but tell the teacher how you did it and make sure the teacher knows it is your work by turning in the notes you took.

My problem is that I have to write a short story and I can't think of one.

Oh, yes you *can*! Think about the last time you forgot to do your homework. Remember how you made up a story about what happened to you and why you didn't get to do the work? That would make a perfectly good short story if you wrote it out.

To write a short story, you can still use the web idea. If you have a hard time getting ideas to start, use the old newspaper writer's trick. Think *who, what, when, where, how,* and *why.*

Who could you write about? *What* were they doing? *When*

did they do it? *Where* were they? *How* did they get out of the situation? *Why* did they do it? You can mix these questions up in any order you want, but if you write out answers to all of them, you have the basis for a good story.

Let's stay with the snowstorm idea. *Who?* Two guys in a snowstorm. *What?* They are trying to rescue a friend who needs to get to the hospital, but his car broke down. *Where?* They are in the ditch with him and the car. *When?* At the height of the snowstorm and all the roads are closed. *Why?* Because they care about him and know he will die if they don't get him to the hospital. *How* do they rescue him? That's your problem! You write the ending.

Suppose I have to write a book report? Would these same ideas work?

Sure. You can use the web idea easily. If the teacher gives you specific questions to answer, just use those for the sen-

tence in the middle of the web. If the teacher just says, "Write a book report," you can combine the ideas we gave you for the short story with the web. Put a sentence about *who* the book is about in the middle of one web, and sentences about *what, when, where, how,* and *why* for other topic sentences.

Take the book *Banner in the Sky*, by James R. Ullman. It is a story about a boy in a blizzard who tries to get to the top of a mountain to redeem his father's honor. The story takes place in the Alps, and it tells how he led the expedition that finally succeeds in getting to the top. Do you see how each of these points could be the topic sentence for a web?

I think I understand. I could use those same ideas in writing a letter, couldn't I? If I wanted to be sure to say everything I wanted to say, I could make up a bunch of webs first.

Right. You could write a great business letter if you use that approach. It is even a good idea if you write your grandmother so you won't forget to thank her for all the things she has sent you.

I get tired of writing. I wish I could do something else.

There are some other things you might do, too. Many times a teacher assigns a written report just so you will do some independent study on a topic. Sometimes a teacher will let you report on your findings by doing a project instead of a written paper.

You will still need to use a plan for gathering your information and you will have to work just as hard, but you might enjoy it more.

Suppose you stick to your topic of snowstorms. You might paint a picture showing the various types of weather fronts involved in a snowstorm. You could visit a weather station and make a slide show of what you saw there. You could take your tape recorder and interview the TV meteorologist on your local TV station. You could even make a weather map for your community, showing where snowstorms come from and what the snowfall has been over the past fifty years.

Use your imagination. Your project could turn out to be the best report you have ever "written."

I've thought about using a typewriter or my parents' computer. Will that help?

Either one could help a lot. If you don't already know how to type, sign up for a course in typing at school as soon as you can. If you use a computer, you will want to use a simple word processing program. Talk to a software dealer. A word processor can take away much of the pain of writing. Rewriting isn't as laborious, so you won't hate doing it.

You will also find that almost everyone writes longer papers when using a word processor than when writing by longhand, and that can help your grades. It will take you some time to learn to use the computer and the word processing system you choose, but from then on you will really save time in preparing papers. You will be amazed at how easy it is to learn. If you do learn to use a computer, you will soon find that you have trouble writing *without* using it.

One other thing—your paper is sure to look neat, and that

often helps grades. If you have a lot of trouble spelling, you may also want to look into getting software that will correct your spelling for you. You will still need to learn to spell, because much of your writing at school (essay tests, for example) cannot be done on the computer, but otherwise the spelling software is great.

I better get started. That research paper I mentioned is due in three weeks. Do you really think I can do it?

We know you can. At best, writing can be exciting. At worst, writing is just a matter of knowing what you want to say and going to the trouble to write it down in a way that makes sense to somebody else.

Don't forget to make your final paper look neat and clean. Teachers tend to give higher grades to papers that look good. Go to an office supply store and look at the various things they sell to help you make papers look neat. They have many kinds of binders and folders. If you tend to make lots of mistakes, they have correction fluid to cover up errors in ink or in typing. They also have correction tape to cover over lines and all kinds of erasers. Shop around and make it easy on yourself.

Someday when you are older and look back through the school papers you have saved, you will enjoy seeing what you wrote. So keep those reports and short stories when you get them back. Give your writing your best shot so you can be proud of it—no matter what your grades.

6
TEST-TAKING TRICKS

People have to take tests all through life. Teachers give tests to find out what kinds of grades to give you and also to find out what kinds of problems you are having. Employers give tests to find out what you are good at doing or whether you can do the job you are applying for. The Department of Motor Vehicles gives tests to find out whether you can be licensed to drive. You just have to get used to the idea of tests.

I hate taking tests. I get nervous and don't do well, even if I know the answers pretty well.

Taking a test makes even the best student nervous. What you need to do is turn that anxiety and the adrenaline it pro-duces into a source of energy to help you do better. Let's talk about what you can do before the test and during it.

The stuff the teacher tells us seems so obvious that I figure I don't need to study until the night before the test.

What you are doing is *cramming*. If you understand all the teacher tells you during class, that means you have a good teacher. You still need to go over the work at night to be able to remember it. But trying to learn everything in *one* night is asking your brain to do the impossible. The more you go over your studies, the more you will remember.

I get confused about how to study for different kinds of tests. Any advice?

You will get three main types of tests in school.

Type 1 includes true-false, multiple choice, and matching. In these tests you will not have to remember the right answer, you will just have to *recognize* it when you see it. This doesn't mean you don't have to study for these; it just means you don't have to spend a lot of time memorizing.

Type 2 includes fill-in-the-blank and essay tests that ask you to list items or give facts. Here you have to know the answer and be able to *recall* it and write it down. You may have to memorize some lists or words that the teacher has said are important. You have to study a little harder.

Type 3 includes the essay questions that ask you to use facts to explain your opinions or ideas about a subject. This requires you to *understand* what you are writing about. You really have to know the material to do well on this kind of test.

How do I know what to study?

If you listen to the teacher, especially the day before the test, he or she will give you all kinds of clues about what will be on the test—sometimes by telling you right out that an item will be on the test, other times by using words like "important," "don't forget," "significant," and so on, giving you hints that the test will touch on these points.

If your test is on a textbook, don't try to read through every chapter. Instead, look at the chapter summaries and the headings in bold-face type. These, plus your notes, often give you most of what you need to know in Type 1 and Type 2 tests. If your test is on something other than your textbook (for instance, a movie, novel, or lecture), you will have to use mainly your notes. If you didn't take good notes, ask a friend if he or she will let you read through their notes. Notes usually let you know what the teacher thought is important.

My social studies teacher lets us use our book and notes for tests in class, so I don't have to study for that test, do I?

You don't have to study the same way you would for a typical closed-book test, but you do have to remember where you can locate the information you need. Searching wastes valuable time; most of your time should be spent answering questions.

A good way to study for an open-book test is to ask yourself questions that might be on the test and then answer them, or at least find the parts of your textbook and notes that will answer them. Remember that familiarity with the material is the key in studying for an open-book test.

Some people find it convenient to use two or three bookmarks in the textbook to help them quickly find very important pages. You don't want to use more than two or three because using too many can be confusing. A good kind of bookmark to use is the little yellow note pads with sticky stuff on the back, which you can get in stationery stores and office supply stores. You can pull them off without messing up your book.

My mom gets after me because I stay up all night studying before a test. I'm just trying to do a good job.

Next to not studying for a test, the worst thing you can do is go into a test situation sleepy, worn out, and nervous from too much coffee the night before.

Studies show that the student who goes into the test rested and relaxed does a better job.

Sure, you will study longer than usual for a test. You need to be prepared. But don't stay up all night!

Some people use studying time to plan how to cheat on a test. Sometimes I think it might be the best way.

There's a good story about a guy who planned to cheat on a history test. He decided to write all the main ideas and dates down on a sheet of paper and hide it in his inside jacket pocket. When he had finished writing it all down, he realized the paper was way too big to go in his pocket, so he got a smaller piece. This time he used many abbreviations and he skipped information that he realized he already knew. Boy, was he disgusted when he found he still had a paper so big it would be obvious he was concealing something. This time he used a really small piece and abbreviated everything—skipping lots of stuff that by now he knew.

The next day he tucked the paper in his jacket, and went off to school. During the morning he put his jacket in his locker to be sure nothing happened to it. Unfortunately, just before history class he was talking to a girl and forgot to get his jacket. His teacher would not let him leave.

Scared, he looked at the test, and to his astonishment it didn't look too hard. He answered all he could and passed with a respectable C+. Why? His repeated writing and reviewing as he prepared his cheat materials was the ideal way to study.

Cheating is cheating. There is no way that it is right. In the long run you will get caught and you will be the one hurt. Don't do it.

Okay. Suppose I'm really prepared. What else should I do the day of the test?

Be sure to get to class on time so you will have plenty of time to get settled, find a pencil and sharpen it, or check to see if your pen writes. Be sure to take an extra pen or pencil.

Try not to talk to other students or listen to them talk about the test. Nothing can get you in a panic worse than hearing some other person say that she memorized all forty-seven of the items on page ninety-two. You probably won't need to know all of them, and if you worry about them, you may get so upset you won't remember what you do know.

Don't forget to go to the restroom before you go into the class. Many teachers will not let you leave during a test, and tension can make you feel the urge to go to the restroom.

Try to cheer up someone else who is upset and anxious. Helping someone else gets your mind off your own worries.

If you are allowed to choose where you sit, a good place is right up front near the teacher. That way you won't be distracted by looking up and seeing other people. You will be able to hear everything the teacher says about how to take the test, and you will also be close enough to ask him or her to explain something if you need help.

So all I need to do now is dive in and write as fast as I can?

Nope. First thing you do is listen *very* carefully to any instructions the teacher gives and read *very* carefully any instructions on the test. We have known students to fail exams, not because they didn't know the answers, but because they didn't follow directions.

When you get the test, skim through the whole thing and budget your time.

How do I do that?

Pay attention to how much each part of the test is worth. Roughly divide the amount of time you have for taking the test among each part of the test. Budgeting time will keep you from spending too much time on any one question and losing points because you never get around to working other parts of the test. Remember, your time budget isn't a math problem that has to be figured to the percentage of a minute. It is just a rough gauge to keep you from leaving out parts of the test—the parts that you might know well and never get to answer because time sneaked up on you.

After I look over the whole test and figure out how I'll budget my time—then what?

Then start right in and keep to the task. Give yourself one or two stretch breaks during the test, but don't let your mind wander.

Do the easiest questions first and then return to the ones that are hardest for you. Sometimes you'll see a word or phrase later in the test that will give you a clue to the answer for another question.

If you don't understand a question, ask the teacher to say it another way or try rewording it yourself. Work until the time is almost up, but try to allow time to check your work.

Should I guess on questions I'm not sure about?

Yes, unless wrong answers will count against you, as in the Scholastic Aptitude Tests (SATs). Avoid wild guesses, though.

You should know that one guess is *not* the same as another. On a multiple choice test made up by your teacher, answers *a* and *d* will rarely be the correct answer. Answers *b* and *c* are your best choices in a four-choice list, and *b*, *c*, or *d* is best in a five-choice list. If one possible answer is much longer than the others, it is very likely correct. But keep in mind that the same letter will probably not be the right answer three times in a row.

On a true-false test, there are usually more false answers. Be very careful with an answer that has two negatives in it, like *not* and *never*. You can get really mixed up. Think of another way to say it. If a statement contains absolutes like

always, *never*, and *all*, the statement is probably false since few things are either true or false *all* the time. If the statement has words like *probably*, *often*, *seldom*, or *most*, the statement is probably true. Do go with your first guess on true-false. It is usually correct.

If time is running out, should I just mark a bunch of answers?

No. On a true-false test, mark all the ones left, false. You will probably have a fifty-fifty chance of getting about half of them right.

On a multiple-choice, mark everything that is left either *b* or *c*. That way you will probably get 20 to 25 percent right.

I have a lot of trouble with machine scored tests where I have a separate answer sheet.

These tests take practice to do well on them. Most people find that it works best to put your test booklet above the answer sheet. If you have a few minutes before the test starts and you are allowed to do so, practice turning the pages easily and marking your answers quickly.

Unless your teacher tells you that you *must not*, a slash mark with a soft pencil is sufficient. You do not need to blacken the whole circle or square completely. That wastes valuable time, and the machine will read the slash mark as well as it reads the whole blacked-in area.

What about essay tests? How do I do those?

Just the words "essay test" strike fear into the hearts of most of us. Essay tests are hard because you not only have to know the content, but you also have to do a lot of on-the-spot thinking. You need to be able to organize the informa-

tion and get your ideas on paper so they can be read and understood by a supercritical someone else. Developing a plan before you start is most helpful.

What do you mean by a plan?

You need to know what you have to do and how you are going to do it. With a plan you are likely to get a better grade than if you just jump in and start writing.

As with any test, first be sure you know exactly what you have to do. If you have to answer only three of the five questions and you answer all five, you will have wasted time and effort.

Next, skim through the test and pick out the questions you will answer and jot down on some scratch paper some notes that come to mind as you see the questions. There's nothing more frustrating than to begin to answer a question and not be able to remember a fact or an idea you had only a few minutes before when you first saw the question.

Here's a question on U.S. history:

Question 1. Discuss the reasons the U.S. developed a policy of isolationism after World War I.

Here's what your notes on scrap paper might look like:

1. People felt all wars unjust. Ocean btwn U.S. and Europe. Bankers made big profits from war. League of Nations didn't work.

Diagramming is another way to make notes. This time look at a question on a novel:

Question 3. Tell how Tom Sawyer felt about going to school and why.

3−	3+
Hated to be inside	Wanted to please aunt
Wanted to be with Huck	Could see Becky

Unless the teacher says you must answer the questions in order, answer the question you feel most confident about first. Just make clear which question you are answering. Very often, answering one question successfully helps you remember information about another question.

If the test is part essay and part objective, glance through the objective part to see if there are any words or phrases in those questions to help you remember something in writing your essay questions.

Remember to watch your time so you can write something on every question, as well as reread what you wrote to be sure you said all you wanted to say the way you wanted to say it.

That seems like so much work, I'll never get the questions answered.

Once you have jotted down the answers in a rough form you can give a sigh of relief and pay attention to the actual writing. That's a lot better than your mind going blank just as you get to the last question! If you do run out of time, turn in the notes or diagram; many teachers will give you partial credit.

Suppose the essay test asks about all the wrong things?

We have all had that happen. Here's what you do. Write down as quickly and carefully as you can what you know about each of the questions on the test. Then write something like this.

"I am sorry, but the questions you asked are not what I studied for. Here is a question I thought you might ask."

Then write a good question and answer it. If the question is on the same material and is a good question, chances are your teacher will give you some credit for it. You cannot do this on every test, but it might pull your grade up enough to get you a pass.

I read and write so slowly that I can't ever finish tests. I know a lot of the answers, but I just can't work fast enough.

You need to talk to each of your teachers and tell them about your problem. Try to get them to give you special permission to take long tests by having someone read them to you and write down the answers for you. It may help if you talk to your counselor or the school reading teacher first and ask them to tell the teachers that you have a real problem.

If you do have someone read the tests to you, be sure to let the person read the question all the way through before you try to answer it. You have seen game shows on TV where the contestant gives the wrong answer because he answered before he heard the full question. If you have any doubt about what the question is, ask the reader to read it again.

If I do all this stuff you have talked about and get a good grade, I'm going to frame it. Usually I can't wait to throw my tests away when I get them back.

We hope you do get a good grade and frame it, but don't throw away old tests—even those with bad grades. Most teachers ask basically the same questions on the semester or end-of-year exams that they did on the short tests leading up to them. Old tests can give you an idea of what the teacher thinks is important. They also can remind you of what you missed and need to study for the final.

I think I will always feel nervous about taking tests.

That's all right. Almost everybody feels that way. Just remember that test-taking is a skill you can learn. The more tests you take, the more confident you will get. In fact, it isn't all bad to be nervous. You want to be nervous enough to keep you alert, but confident enough to feel sure you can do a good job. And you can do a good job. Just study, be cool in the test situation, and do your best. You will do just fine.

7
HOW TO
GET HELP

If your folks are in the middle of a messy divorce or your dad just lost his job, it is hard to study.

If you are in a school where some of your friends are pushing you to "get" certain teachers, it is hard to work on a history report.

If everything in your life seems all wrong and you are wondering about suicide, the English class word list doesn't seem to matter.

Whatever your problem is, *don't give up. Get help now.*

The worst thing you can do is to start messing up in school, hoping (consciously or unconsciously) that someone will notice that you are in trouble and help you. What is more likely to happen is that people will fuss and yell at you and make things worse for you.

Turning to drugs or drink or living dangerously are terrible ways to call attention to your problems. They hurt you most of all, and you don't deserve to be hurt—no matter what you have done or think you have done. We all do rotten things, but we can live them down. Drink, drugs, and wild driving only bring on more problems.

You must choose what you do about your problems. You can be smart and get help; there are many places where you can get support and counsel, whatever your problem.

Even though it is sometimes hard to believe, other people do need you and care about you. Reach out and let someone know you need help.

Important. Many phone books list all kinds of numbers to call for help in the first two or three pages. Look there first. If you have to look up the number of an agency, don't look in the listings with people's names or the yellow pages. Look in the section for businesses or in the section for government agencies. Ask a friendly teacher to help you find numbers you need. Below are listed some special problems and some places to look for help.

Suicide. You feel that dying would help.

Get help *now*, please.

- *Call a local hotline or suicide prevention number. Keep calling until you get someone. Be honest.*
- *Call your family doctor or local public health clinic.*
- *Tell someone in your family. Make them know you are serious.*
- *Talk to your school counselor or psychologist.*
- *Go to the emergency room at the hospital.*
- *Talk to someone, anyone. Don't give up. Help is there.*

Normal Family Problems (disagreements over bedtime, when to get home at night, a room of your own, friends, etc.)

- *Talk to your parents honestly—when you are not mad and upset. This helps more often than you think.*
- *Talk to a school counselor or a favorite teacher. Ask them to talk with you and your folks together.*
- *Join a youth group at a church or temple. They talk about problems like this. So do many teen clubs. It helps to learn you are not alone.*
- *Talk to another relative—aunt, uncle, grandparent. Ask them what can be done.*
- *Go to the library and talk to the librarian. There are several good books for teenagers on how to get along with parents.*

Serious Family Problems (physical abuse, sexual abuse, divorce, abandonment, criminal or racial threats to family safety, illness, money, etc.)

- *Talk to someone in the family you can trust and find out if anything is being done. You don't want to make things worse. Ask how you can help.*
- *Call the main number for county offices and ask the operator who answers to connect you with a family service agency.*
- *Call the state public assistance phone number and ask for help.*
- *Go to any minister or rabbi and tell them the problem and ask where you can go for help.*
- *Call the police department and ask for protective services if you feel your life is in danger.*

Bullying, Shakedowns, Physical Threats from Other Teenagers

- *If it takes place at school, go to the principal.*
- *If the school can't or won't handle it, call the police in the area where it happens. Make sure you have your facts straight—dates, times, names, descriptions, etc.*
- *Let your parents know.*
- *Don't try to handle it with just your friends. It may get worse.*

Dating and Social Problems

- *Join a teen club, Y program, scouting, or religious youth group. Many of these groups have people to advise you. They are also great places to meet new friends.*
- *Talk to your parents. They can help more than you think.*
- *Talk to your school counselor about setting up a peer group at school to talk about teen problems.*

Emotional Problems (feel like you are going crazy, death of one of your folks, death of a brother or sister, someone in family slowly dying)

- *Talk to your family physician or go to a public health clinic.*
- *Talk to a school psychologist.*
- *Talk to a minister or rabbi.*
- *If your brother or sister has cancer, call your local American Cancer Society and ask for the booklet "When Your Sister or Brother Has Cancer."*
- *If your brother or sister dies, get in touch with a group called Compassionate Friends (P.O. Box 1347, Oakbrook, IL 60521. Phone 312 323-5010). They can help you with your grief.*
- *Call a hotline and talk to someone about referring you to a counselor.*

- *Talk to your folks about how you feel. If you can't talk to them, talk to your grandparents, aunt, or uncle.*
- *Talk to your school counselor and get help in making up work if you have to miss a lot of school.*

Drug and Alcohol Problems

- *Get in touch with your family doctor or local health clinic. Remember, not all doctors know how to treat alcohol and drug problems. If you don't get help, call and talk to someone at Alcoholics Anonymous and ask for the names of some doctors who can help.*
- *Call Alcoholics Anonymous and Alateen. These are listed in the phone book, sometimes under AA.*
- *Call a local hotline and ask for the number of a local group that works with drug rehabilitation.*
- *Believe what they tell you about drug and alcohol abuse being a sickness that can be helped.*

Problems of Pregnancy, Venereal Disease, Other Health Concerns

- *If at all possible, go to your parents first. They are likely to be more understanding than you think they will be.*
- *Talk to your school nurse if you have one.*
- *Go to your family doctor or the local health clinic.*
- *Call the local hotline number for names of special clinics and health services for your problem.*
- *Remember, by law, schoolteachers in many states may not be allowed to talk with you about sexual problems, so don't be upset if they refuse. Go somewhere else.*

Running Away

- *Try to solve your problems. Running away won't help except for the moment.*
- *If you need to get away for a while, ask your parents to let you stay with a friend or relative until you feel better about your problems.*
- *Don't try to stay at a friend's house without telling the friend's parents that you are running away. You might get them in trouble with the law for taking you in.*
- *If you do run, plan to go to a shelter for runaways. Many towns and cities have them. Many young people who try*

to live on the street get raped, killed, or at least badly hurt by older street people.

- *Put this toll-free number in your pocket: 1 800 621-4000. This is the National Runaway Switchboard. They will help you find food, clothing, and shelter. They will even contact your parents if you want them to, without telling where you are. Another Runaway number is 1 800 231-6946 (in Texas it is 1 800 392-3352). Do send some kind of message to your folks. They care, even if they don't show it.*

> WHEN I RAN AWAY I CALLED THE NATIONAL RUNAWAY SWITCHBOARD. 1-800-621-4000. THEY GOT ME FOOD AND SHELTER. THEY EVEN CONTACTED MY PARENTS WITHOUT TELLING THEM WHERE I WAS. TRUTH WAS, I DIDN'T WANT TO SEE MY PARENTS THEN, BUT I ALSO DIDN'T WANT THEM TO WORRY!

- *If you have no money and want to go home, go to the nearest police station and tell them you want to use Trailways Bus Company's Operation Free. Once they are sure you are on the level, Trailways will give you a free bus ticket home. Remember, go to the police station first, not the bus station.*

Problems Stemming from Racial, Ethnic, or Sexual Prejudice

- *Talk to your school principal or counselor. Have facts, dates, times, etc.*
- *Try to find a local human relations group. Call a local hotline or your local government to find out the number.*
- *Go to a legal aid clinic, or call a lawyer if you can afford to pay for one.*

ACLD NATIONAL HEADQUARTERS,
4156 LIBRARY RD.,
PITTSBURGH
PA. 15234

← GREAT FOR INFORMATION ON LEARNING DISABILITIES.

Reading and Writing Problems—Learning Disabilities

- *Talk to your counselor or the school reading teacher. Tell them exactly what problems you are having.*
- *Get a tutor. If you can't pay one, offer to trade a service like car washing or house cleaning for lessons. Most schools have a list of tutors.*
- *For more information on learning disabilities, write to ACLD National Headquarters, 4156 Library Rd., Pittsburgh, PA 15234. You may be able to find a local chapter.*
- *For special help with reading problems (dyslexia), write to the Orton Society, 8415 Bellona Lane, Towson, MD 21204.*

Problems of Tension, Stress, Nerves, Fatigue

- *If the problem persists, go to your doctor or to a health clinic.*
- *Join a class in yoga, meditation, or relaxation.*
- *Join a religious group.*
- *Get a book or tape on relaxation. Ask the librarian for one.*

Some Other Problem?

There are many other kinds of problems. If this list did not include yours, use some of the resources listed, like the hotlines, to find someplace to go for help.

Don't be shy about asking. Don't be ashamed because of something you did. Somewhere out there, there is someone who can help you. You just have to keep trying. The first people you turn to may not help. Don't let that stop you. Try again and again until you get help.

If your problems are keeping you from doing well in school, taking care of them is just about the most important thing you can do.

To stay in school, to learn, to graduate someday—these are major goals for you at this time of your life. They take hard work and concentration. But the payoff in good feelings about yourself will make it all worth the effort.

Believe it. You can make it. Hang in there. You don't have to drop out.

INDEX